LET ALL THE PEOPLES PRAISE HIM

Michel de Verteuil

Let all the peoples praise him

Lectio Divina and the Psalms

the columba press

First published in 2000 by
the columba press
55A Spruce Avenue, Stillorgan Industrial Park,
Blackrock, Co Dublin

Reprinted 2001

Cover by Bill Bolger
Origination by The Columba Press
Printed in Ireland by Colour Books Ltd, Dublin

ISBN 1 85607 231 2

Quotations from the Psalms are taken from The Grail Psalms,
copyright © The Grail (England) 1963 and are used by permission.

Contents

Foreword

One of the goals set for the church by the Second Vatican Council was that the psalms should become the personal prayer of its members. There has been some headway towards achieving this goal – many lay people now pray *The Prayer of the Church* on a regular basis – but there is still some way to go. This little book is intended as a modest contribution to continuing the journey.

We must understand what is implied in making the psalms our personal prayer. It means first of all praying the psalms because we like them, not primarily to fulfil an obligation, as clerics, religious, or members of a community. We look to the day when the psalter will become the prayer book of the Christian people, carried around in pockets, briefcases and handbags, as we do with our rosaries and devotional books.

It also means praying many of the psalms, not merely the 'old faithfuls' like the Good Shepherd psalm or the *De Profundis*. We may not come to the point of praying the entire 150, but we certainly need to extend our repertoire more widely than at present.

Finally, we must go further than praying one line of a psalm, which is often presented as the high point of psalm praying. We must learn to pray the psalms in their entirety, as we do with our devotional prayers, entering into each one's movement of thought and grasping its logic. Only then will the psalms become a school of spirituality. It is true, as we shall see in chapter 4, that we eventually find ourselves focusing on one line, but this should normally happen only after we have prayed the whole psalm.

The method I advocate in this book is *lectio divina*. I have explained in chapter 4 how the method works, but because it is basic to the book, I have included a brief summary on page 9.

The book is intended primarily for those who have neither time nor inclination for academic study, and therefore I have included very little background information on the psalms. This is in no way to suggest that Bible study cannot be a help to prayer; it certainly can, and should lead to deepening one's prayer life. I learnt this many years ago, when I studied at the University of Fribourg in Switzerland under teachers who were both Bible scholars and spiritual guides.

The condition is that we must always be relating Bible text and experience, allowing each to enrich the other – as in the *lectio* method. We must stress also that those who do not have the opportunity for deep study can attain a deep understanding and love of the psalms – as indeed of the whole Bible.

Even small books are a collaborative effort. This one would not have seen the light of day without my friend and colleague in the *lectio divina* apostolate in Dublin, Elena Lombardi-French. She first conceived the project, transcribed tapes of seven lectures on the psalms I had given in my native Trinidad, and then continued to encourage me as I adapted the material from the spoken to the written word.

We have been guided by the common goal of ministering in Jesus' name to the many people who still call on him, 'Lord, teach us to pray' (Lk 11:1).

The Method of Lectio Divina

Lectio divina is a method of meditative Bible reading which goes back to the early centuries of our church, and continues to be a source of deep spiritual growth.

Lectio divina (a Latin expression which means 'sacred reading') is done in three stages:

Reading: You read the passage slowly and reverentially, allowing the words to sink into your consciousness. If necessary you clarify the meaning of words or expressions that you are not familiar with.

Meditation: You allow the passage to stir up memories within you so that you recognise in it your own experience or that of people who have touched your life.

Prayer: You allow the meditation to lead you to prayer – thanksgiving, humility and petition.

Note on Translations and Numbering

The texts in this book use the translation of the psalms found in most English editions of *The Prayer of the Church*. Called popularly 'the Grail Version', it was published in England in 1963. This translation was chosen because the method of *lectio divina* requires that we use the same text for both personal meditation and community prayer.

I have followed the numbering of the psalms normally used in Bibles, which is different from that of the church's liturgical books. From psalms 11 to 145, the number in Bibles is one more than in the liturgical books. Psalm 9 in the liturgical books is divided into two in Bibles, and numbered 9 and 10. On the other hand, 146 and 147 in the liturgical books are one in the Bibles, numbered 147. The difference in numbering is to be traced back to the two established versions of the Old Testament texts. The liturgical books follow the Greek translation of the Bible called the *Septuagint*, whereas most popular Bibles follow the Hebrew texts.

CHAPTER 1

The Psalms as a School of Spirituality

In recent years, many Catholics have taken to praying the psalms as their personal prayer. The psalms have become, in fact as well as in name, the prayer of the church, not merely of priests and religious as was the case for many centuries.

Making the psalms our personal prayer is a big step, however. Those who decide to take this step will have to overcome many obstacles and the purpose of this little book is to help them do so. One area that must be looked at very carefully is spirituality, which can be loosely defined as the way we relate with God and the transcendent.

The Second Vatican Council raised the issue of different spiritualities in our church, notably in article 13 of the *Decree on the Liturgy,* which dealt with 'private devotions'. This expression referred to the many religious practices which are not part of the liturgy but play a very important part in the life of the church – the rosary, the prayers of sodalities, the angelus, novenas, pilgrimages, processions, etc.

Article 13 says first that these devotions are to be commended but then adds that they 'should be so drawn up that they harmonise with the liturgical seasons, accord with the sacred liturgy, are in some fashion derived from it, and lead people to it, since the liturgy by its very nature, far surpasses any of them'.

As the text indicates, the council fathers felt there was need to correct a problem in the church – the spirituality of the 'devotions' was not always in harmony with that of the liturgy.

The church has always recognised different schools of spirituality within its tradition. They have generally been categorised according to the great religious orders – Benedictine, Dominican, Franciscan, Carmelite and so on. The council invites us to go beyond these categories and ask a more fundamental question: Is a spirituality 'in accord with' the sacred liturgy? Is it 'in some fashion derived from it'?

That the question is important is brought out by an old adage of our church, *lex orandi, lex credendi,* 'the law of prayer is the law of faith'. The adage is saying that there is an inter-relationship between our prayer and our faith – taken in the widest sense of our entire relationship with God, and therefore includes our spirituality. The way we pray expresses and nourishes our spirituality. We can conclude that by praying with the liturgy (which means in practice with the Bible) we will develop a biblical spirituality.

For many centuries now, the liturgy was not a source of spirituality. The Bible wasn't either, since even when it was read, it was not a book of prayer. People went to Mass, and did so with love and very great reverence, but their spirituality was nourished not by the prayers of the Mass but by their personal devotions.

In fact, many people practised their devotions during Mass. While the priest said the prayers of the Mass, they prayed the rosary and other prayers they were committed to. Priests too, having celebrated Mass and said the divine office, felt the need to supplement these with personal devotions.

The Constitution on the Sacred Liturgy aimed to correct this situation when it said: 'Because it is the public prayer of the church, the divine office is a source of piety and nourishment for personal prayer' (90), adding the exhortation: 'Priests and all of those who take part in the divine office are earnestly exhorted in the Lord to attune their minds to their voices when praying it.' It then drew the conclusion: 'The better to achieve this ideal, let them take steps to improve their understanding of the liturgy and of the Bible, especially the psalms.'

According to the teaching of the Council, therefore, it is not enough to read the psalms; we have to 'attune our minds' to them – enter their spirituality.

A very beautiful passage from *Dei Verbum,* the conciliar document on the Bible, makes the same point: 'In the sacred books, the Father who is in heaven meets his children with great love and speaks with them. The force and the power in the Word of God is so great that it remains the support and energy of the church, the strength of faith for her children, the food of the soul, and the pure and perennial source of spiritual life' (21).

We read the psalms for different reasons. Sometimes we turn to them for moral teaching: 'The psalms say we should do this, so we should do it.' At other times we look for something comforting or soothing. The words are so beautiful, or so familiar ('The Lord is my shepherd, there is nothing I shall want') that reciting them gives us comfort and consolation.

These purposes are not sufficient today. We must read the psalms because the law of prayer is the law of faith – by praying them we will enter into their spirituality.

This will not happen, however, unless we are conscious of the kind of spirituality they express and nourish, the history of this spirituality and in particular why it was neglected in recent centuries, and how it is different from the spirituality of the devotions. To pray the psalms at this point in the history of the church is a conversion which we must enter into consciously. We must come to the psalms anxious to embrace their spirituality.

In Deuteronomy 4:6, Moses says that the gentiles will one day exclaim: 'What nation is there that has laws and customs that match this whole Law!' We are those gentiles who recognise that the psalms present us with a 'Law' which cannot be 'matched'. More than that, by praying them, the 'whole Law' which Moses handed down to his descendants becomes ours.

CHAPTER 2

Parallelism

Having decided that we are going to read the psalms for our personal prayer (and therefore as spiritual nourishment), we will have to adapt ourselves to their style of praying. We look first at one aspect of their style – parallelism.

The psalms are poetry and, like all poetry, have rhythm. In many languages the rhythm of poetry consists of beat and rhyme; the rhythm of Hebrew poetry is parallelism – sentences are divided into sections with each one echoing the other. Parallelism is found right through the Bible, but most notably in the psalms. We must, therefore, understand parallelism and become familiar with it so that we can be comfortable in using it in the psalms.

We can distinguish three kinds of parallelism in the psalms. The first we can call 'synonymous', where there is almost no difference between what the two halves of the sentence are saying. A very well known example is the invocation we use at the beginning of many prayers, 'O God, come to our assistance, O Lord, make haste to help us.'

Other examples are: 'Hear this all you peoples, give heed all you who dwell in the world'; 'men both low and high, rich and poor alike'; 'My lips will speak words of wisdom, my heart is full of insight'; 'I remembered my God and I groaned, I pondered and my spirit fainted' ; 'Zion hears and is glad, the people of Judah rejoice'.

Secondly, there is 'antithetic' parallelism, where one half of the sentence says the opposite of the other. 'Some trust in chariots and horses, but we in the name of the Lord; they will collapse and fall, but we shall stand firm' (20:7-8).

A third form, very beautiful and touching, is 'progressive' parallelism. The psalm says something once and then says it again, but with a slight difference, and sometimes a third time, with a slight difference again. This is not repetition since each line adds something new – the thought progresses, even though slowly.

An example is 29:1-2: 'O give the Lord, you sons of God, give the Lord glory and power, give the Lord the glory of his name.' The thought progresses, a little bit at a time. So too: 'O sing a new song to the Lord – sing to the Lord all the earth – sing to the Lord bless his name' (96:1). Quite frequently there is the progression from 'the sons of Israel' to the 'sons of Aaron' to 'those who fear the Lord', for example, in 118:2-4.

An outstanding example of progressive parallelism is the whole of psalm 119, a prolonged meditation on 'the law of God', which must be broadly interpreted to mean God's will in all its forms. Every verse or group of verses speaks of a different aspect of the greatness and the beauty of God's law. The psalm becomes a leisurely, meditative walk through the complexity and mystery of God's will.

One great advantage of parallelism is that it is not merely a very beautiful form of poetry, but, unlike beat and rhyme, it is translatable from one language to another.

More importantly, however, parallelism is a style of prayer that is unhurried. It fits well into Jesus' teaching that prayer is not passing information on to God, since he already knows not merely our needs but all our inmost thoughts. Prayer is getting in touch with the truth of ourselves.

We need to remember this very specially today. Our culture is all oriented towards achievement and this has affected our prayer, which often becomes busy and self-important. The psalms, with their parallelism, teach us to pray as Jesus taught, to remember that knocking at the door is the important thing, because once we have knocked, it has already been opened.

CHAPTER 3

Praying with the Imagination

The psalms teach us to pray in imaginative language.

The psalmist is under attack: 'Many bulls have surrounded me, fierce bulls of Bashan close me in, against me they open wide their jaws, like lions, rending and roaring' (22:12-13). He is afraid: 'Like water I am poured out, disjointed are all my bones, my heart has become like wax, it is melted within my breast' (22:15), 'an army is encamped against me' (27:3). He has experienced God's grace: 'He drew me from the deadly pit, from the miry clay' (40:3), or God's power: 'The Lord shatters the cedars of Lebanon, he makes Lebanon leap like a calf' (29:5).

Imaginative praying is difficult for us. Our culture is rational; we feel secure when communication is clear, when we can explain, understand – and control – it. In fact, our church culture considers the imagination dangerous, like a wayward child we cannot trust, and which must be controlled. This is specially important when it comes to doctrines. What we call in our tradition 'an act of faith', is expressed in very precise language. God must not be left in any doubt about what we believe – three persons in one God, seven sacraments, Jesus really present, 'body, blood, soul and divinity'.

We prefer to pray in that way too, in clear, objective language, which leaves no room for ambiguity – neither on our part nor on God's. 'Lord, I have an English examination tomorrow, and I want you to help me with it. Not the maths, that I can handle; it's the English.' We tell God that our eldest son (not the younger one) is causing us trouble. Often when people ask us priests to pray for an intention, they have the name written down, or ask us to write it out, making sure we get the spelling right.

There is something very touching about this insistence that we make our prayers specific – God's people at home with him, like teenagers making sure that their parents understand their language. But it brings out the point that we are not accustomed to praying imaginatively. When we want to deepen our prayer life too, we speak of 'going beyond images' – imaginative prayer is looked on as inferior.

Praying imaginatively will not come naturally to us; therefore, we must choose to do it and this requires that we be convinced it is worth doing, that it is in fact the way of our church tradition. It sets us free, with the freedom of God's sons and daughters which Jesus won back for us.

Imaginative praying frees us first from the control of reason and will. These faculties are necessary for mature living, but they also keep us in bondage to prejudices, irrational guilt and fear. They prevent us stepping out in new directions and taking chances so that we can re-examine old positions.

The psalms invite us to let memories come to our consciousness uncensored. Our upbringing tells us that we shouldn't mention certain things in God's presence – we shouldn't tell him about our anger, or ask him for certain things. In imaginative praying, such as when we pray the psalms, we don't censor. We pour out our anger before God, tell him of our longings, and ask him why he is so slow to answer. We trust that if we are saying the wrong thing, we will see the error of our ways when it is right for us.

Imaginative praying also frees us from isolation. One of our greatest sufferings, in our relationship with one another and with God, is the feeling that we are alone, the only ones who ever committed this sin, or experienced this humiliation. Jesus, however, has drawn all humanity to himself as he promised. Nothing we go through should isolate us. Others have gone that way before us and are doing so now – thanking, begging for forgiveness and salvation in all its forms.

Through imaginative praying, the psalms invite us to move beyond our individual experience and enter into this universal communion. Like all great works of art, they are both concrete enough to touch our imaginations and adaptable to many different situations. We can pray them both personally and collectively. A psalm of lamentation, for example, leads us into communion with all those who are mourning, today and in the past, praying in and with us.

We call the divine office *The Prayer of the Church,* not merely because it is the church's official prayer but because the whole church is praying in communion – through imaginative praying.

We experience Jesus praying with us too. The psalms express what he felt in the depth of himself and so praying them leads us to know him better. The epistle to the Hebrews says: 'It is not as if we had a high priest who was incapable of feeling our weaknesses with us; we have one who has been tempted in every way that we are, though he is without sin' (4:15). Jesus prayed the psalms, and we should pray them in the consciousness that he is living his earthly life in us now. He is seated at the right hand of the Father but prays in and with us (cf. Jn 14:20).

Imaginative praying frees us from bondage to the particular text. The source of all misinterpretations of the Christian message is people limiting themselves to one text, with its one metaphor and one experience of God. They do not, with the rest of the church, experience communion with other texts, metaphors and experiences.

We avoid that trap when we pray the psalms imaginatively and are, therefore, not in bondage to any one metaphor. In some psalms, God comes across as a warrior, condoning (even ordering) violence, but then we move to others where he is a mother, forgiving and merciful. We are able to find solace or be challenged in whatever situation we find ourselves.

The Rule of St Benedict, which is founded on the spirituality of the Bible, in particular of the psalms, describes the

prayer of the monks like this: *Magnificant Dominum in se op-
erantem*, 'They glorify the Lord at work in themselves.' That
is what we do when we pray the psalms, not merely in thanksgiving but in petition, repentance, trust.

The words *in se* mean literally 'in themselves', but as always
in Latin, a simple expression must be given a wide interpretation. It means 'in their entire life experience' – in the world,
nature, the whole history of humanity. We can enter into that
only if we pray imaginatively.

Note the expression, 'glorify the Lord,' taken from the
Magnificat. When we pray the psalms, we pray as Mary prayed;
she prays in us. This explains our Catholic tradition of saying
the *Magnificat* each evening. We remember the ways in which
on that day we have experienced that 'the Lord has looked on
our lowliness'.

The *Magnificat* comes at the end of evening prayer, sum-
ming up how we have prayed the psalms, indeed all the
prayers we have said that day.

CHAPTER 4

Objective and Subjective Prayer

Praying the psalms involves being both objective and subjective, with each aspect complementing the other.

When we come to pray a psalm we must first be objective. Every psalm has its own character, its mood, its movement of thought; we must observe it, take stock of it, respect it, let it be itself. We must make sure to get to the feelings which the psalm expresses. Here and now, we might not share these feelings, but we accept them.

This need for objectivity explains our old church tradition of chanting the psalms; it is a way of respecting their identity.

Our aim should be to pray the entire psalm as a unit – not necessarily the first time we read it. If, here and now, we can take in only a few verses at a time, one line even, we can be content with that for the time being. But to stay there (as many are inclined to do) is not doing justice to the psalm which was composed and handed down as one prayer. It is particularly important that we get accustomed to the psalmist's unstructured, spontaneous way of prayer.

We must also let praying a psalm become a subjective experience. We allow it to touch us – not our minds but our feelings. We identify with it so that it becomes our personal prayer. As I said, we may not be experiencing the feelings here and now. In that case, we remember a time when we did, and then pray the psalm as a memory. Or then we identify with another person or group who is going through the experience and pray the psalm with them or, better, let them pray through us.

There is a spirituality involved here. It says that our state of mind – sadness, gratitude, compassion for others – is our opening to God, the gate by which we enter his presence. Cardinal Hume once said: 'We find our way to God through our humanity, and not despite it.' This is the spirituality fostered by the psalms. By entering into the truth of who we (or others) are, we meet God. If we are angry, we let ourselves be angry in the presence of God.

The best way to achieve the combination of objectivity and subjectivity in praying the psalms is through *lectio divina,* sacred or meditative reading. This is the oldest method of Bible reading in our Catholic tradition, having been systematised some time around the fifth century. It is a simple but very deep method, specially suited to the psalms.

In *lectio divina,* we read the psalm in three stages – reading, meditation and prayer.

At the first stage – reading – we take the objective approach. We read the psalm, from beginning to end, slowly and meditatively. We get the meaning of the words (making enquiries if necessary), follow the movement of thought, accustom ourselves to the sound of the words so that they resonate in us.

At the meditation stage we become subjective. We situate ourselves in the psalm, become conscious of what's in our heart at this moment, how the psalm fits our personal experience. If necessary we remember the past or get in touch with others as explained above.

It is to be noted, by the way, that the meditation stage of *lectio divina* is different from the exercise which goes by that name in other prayer methods. In *lectio divina,* meditation is a moment of activity, interior but activity none the less.

We then move spontaneously to the third stage, when the combination of objectivity and subjectivity leads to prayer. We recite the psalm as our personal heartfelt prayer, coming from our experience.

We recite the whole psalm prayerfully, but as our prayer gets deeper we will feel ourselves specially touched by one verse. When this happens we continue repeating the verse until we find ourselves resting in it; it becomes part of us even when we start doing other things, going out for a walk, taking the bus, or setting about household duties. We have then moved into contemplative prayer. We eventually come to the point where we say the words, not verbally but in an unspoken way, from within our hearts.

CHAPTER 5

Choosing a Psalm

How do we pick the psalm we're going to pray? The question is important. How we pick our psalms will reflect and foster our understanding of prayer and, therefore, our spirituality.

Our Catholic tradition gives us two methods of choosing a psalm. The first is to choose one which suits our present state – soothes our pain, gives us new courage, expresses our joy. The index provided in some psalm books is intended to guide our choice. Psalms are listed as appropriate for times of desolation, joy, success and so on.

The more common tradition in our church, however, is that the psalms are arranged in a book (the 'breviary' or 'little book') according to a pattern arranged over a certain period, one week, or four weeks as it has been since the Second Vatican Council.

Whatever the arrangement, we say a psalm not because we have chosen it but because it is the one we find in the church's prayer book. We must then decide that we will let it speak to our situation. For example, we meet a psalm which is the prayer of a person in distress, so we get in touch with our feelings of distress and say the psalm from there. Or then we say, 'I am not in distress at present, but I will think of someone who is,' – a member of my family, a friend, someone I read about in the papers or saw on TV – and I decide to say the psalm with them. As was explained in the previous chapter, the imaginative language of the psalms makes this possible.

This method of choosing the psalm we pray is spiritually healthy. It takes us out of the individualism of our culture and makes us experience our communion with others – family and friends, the church, all humanity, at the deepest level with Jesus himself, allowing him to pray with and in us.

There were times when the church was insistent that all 150 psalms must be said. This was based on the idea that saying all the psalms brings automatic blessings. This custom has not been followed, however – in the present breviary some are left out.

Even with the present arrangement, we should not be scrupulous about reading all the psalms prescribed. At the beginning, we will be able to do very few at a time, so we pick one, and let that suffice for that day – although we might try another in the evening. So there are two principles at work. We don't hurry our psalm praying, we do it slowly and meditatively. On the other hand, it is essential to the method of psalm praying that we don't remain with one psalm, but pray a variety of them, entering into their spirituality.

One mistake is to pray too many psalms, the other to remain with one alone. We work out our own rhythm. Gradually we get to love more and more of them, eventually the 150 – if the Lord lets us live long enough.

Once we have chosen the psalm we are going to pray, our next task is to discern what kind of psalm it is.

The psalms can be categorised subjectively – who is praying or being prayed for – and objectively, by content. Subjectively, there are three kinds of psalm: prayers of (or for) an individual, a nation or a king. Psalms 86, 136, and 143 are examples of individual psalms; 85 is a prayer of the nation; 72 and 101 are prayers for the king.

Objectively, we divide the psalms according to the situation out of which the psalmist is praying. Scholars propose different ways of dividing them, but my experience is that they can all be accommodated in three categories: lament, praise, and wisdom. Psalms of lament come from a situation of suffering, psalms of praise from a situation of victory, wisdom psalms are reflections on life. The appendix on page 63 gives a list of the psalms in these categories.

Having made these distinctions, we must add immediately that the psalms cannot be fitted neatly into categories. They differ from our usual prayers in this way. In the Catholic Church, from our earliest years we learnt to make different 'acts' – of repentance, faith, thanksgiving, petition. Each 'act' is a clearly distinct kind of prayer. It was popular at one time to teach the various aspects of prayer through the acronym ACTS – adoration, contrition, thanksgiving, supplication.

I find that prayer groups today continue the practice of making a clear distinction between different categories of prayer. There are fixed times for each category and they must be adhered to; one is not permitted to make a prayer of thanksgiving when it is time for petitions, or repentance when it is time for praise. So, too, we have always been taught to be clear about who we are praying for – we prefer to name the person or group.

The psalms are different. They cannot be categorised strictly, and the reason is simply that they came out of particular experiences, and our human response to an experience is always complex. We move from one feeling to another. We are praying for the country, and we suddenly realise that we are praying for ourselves; we are praying for ourselves and then we realise that it's our children we're praying for.

The psalms are spontaneous like that. Psalm 131, for example, starts with two personal stanzas, then verse three says, 'O Israel, hope in the Lord...' Is it a person or the nation that is praying? The psalmist would probably answer that he wasn't thinking along those lines at all. He was letting his prayer flow naturally and spontaneously.

In praying the psalms we, too, can be very free. The general principle is that we can pray any psalm either personally or collectively. 'Israel' can be our community or country, but it can also be ourselves or someone we would like to pray for. 'The just one' can be someone we admire but it can also be a good family or an ideal community.

We can also be free in interpreting the various titles.

'Priests of the Lord' are those who bring holiness into the world. 'The Egyptians' are the forces which block the work of God. 'The King' is any one exercising authority in a community, no matter how small – family, neighbourhood, parish, classroom.

As regards content, the psalms are also fluid – like life. A psalm of lament turns to petition, praise becomes a meditation on life, hope suddenly turns to despair, insecurity to confidence, envy to compassion.

Psalm 85 can serve as an example. Verses 2-8 are a prayer in a time of suffering. The psalmist challenges the Lord, asking him why has he allowed this: 'You have once favoured your land; you revived the fortunes of Jacob.' Then he turns to petition: 'Revive us now, God our helper; will you be angry with us forever?' In verse 9 the mood changes again, things are going to be all right: 'The Lord will make us prosper; our earth shall yield its fruit; justice shall march before him and peace shall follow his steps.'

By entering into these 'mood swings' of the psalms, our prayer becomes more spontaneous, freer, more in accord with the truth of our feelings. This is one of the most precious fruits of praying the psalms.

CHAPTER 6

Psalms of Lament

The psalms of lament are a very deep form of prayer. Jesus prayed them, so did Mary, and the church has always prayed them.

Many people don't like these psalms, indeed are turned off praying the psalms altogether because of them. They find that the psalmist is a chronic complainer, always going on about how unfair life is. Why can't he, like the rest of us, stop complaining and make the best of things?

The problem is that our style of praying and, at a deeper level, our spirituality are not sufficiently biblical – for the very good reason that we don't pray with the Bible. Rather than giving up on the psalms of lament, we must therefore learn how to pray them in accord with our Catholic spiritual tradition. We will eventually grow to love them, and they will convert us, lead us to the heart of biblical spirituality, New and Old Testaments, the spirituality of Jesus himself.

The psalms of lament are prayers of petition, based on situations in which the psalmists find themselves. They tell concretely and dramatically, but always in imaginative language as we have seen, the story of human suffering, the common destiny we all share.

There is physical pain first of all, often expressed in the image of drowning (e.g. 88:8, 18), or of being overwhelmed. There is also the image of fever, our body feeling as if it is on fire, our bones like wax or water (e.g. 22:15) so that we cannot hold ourselves straight.

The psalmist's sufferings are more painful since they are inflicted by others. This introduces the theme of 'the enemies', so prominent in these psalms. The psalmist goes into detail about his enemies; they plot (e.g. 83:4), or set traps (e.g. 27:11), meaning that they are conscious of the harm they are doing. They taunt shamelessly as if they have no fear of God (e.g. 7:10-12), or do not realise that their deceitfulness will come to light one day.

The psalms of lament also speak of inner sufferings, remorse, resentment, humiliation, the sense of failure.

In reading these psalms we allow the concrete language to evoke memories. These can be personal – a time when we had a roasting fever which left us weak or when someone we loved let us down. But they can evoke memories of others, of television pictures we saw the previous night: civil war in Algeria; a cyclone in Bangladesh; AIDS in Uganda; cholera in Peru. We may have been to a hospital recently and seen patients suffering. The psalm then becomes the prayer of suffering humanity – ourselves, others, our communities and nations, the human family.

The psalmist does not relate his sufferings in a dispassionate way. He is angry about them and especially at his enemies. This poses a problem for us because, according to the teaching of Jesus, we dare not adopt a self-righteous or condemning attitude in our prayer.

There are various strategies we can adopt to avoid that trap. One is to focus not on individuals but on forces or tendencies. We think of evil elements of our culture, for example, greed, racism, addictions, hypocrisy, fanaticism, sexism. The words of the psalms are very true of these things – they are pervasive, 'on every side'; the evil they do is not accidental, they are 'plotting', 'waiting in ambush'; they are insidious and hide behind nice language, 'all honey their speech'.

We can also think of evil tendencies within individuals, ourselves and others – addiction to drink or drugs, for example, depression, lack of self-confidence. These things 'lie in wait' for us; if we drop our guard, they move in on us. We think of habitual personal sins such as pride, lust, jealousy, lack of forgiveness. These too are 'enemies' that leave us feeling weary and discouraged. We plead with God to deliver us from them.

There will be times when we remember personal 'enemies' – those who have betrayed our confidence, abused us in our home, humiliated us in the workplace. The psalms of lament then become the expression of our hurt, anger or resentment. Here especially we must be careful to avoid self-righteousness, however. One way is to remember how we too have been 'enemies' to others – or to ourselves. We too 'lie in wait,' taunt, plot, often in subtle ways. We then ask God to defeat all 'enemies' – including ourselves.

The psalms of lament pose a problem for us because our culture, both in society and in church, does not encourage us to acknowledge anger. Modern pop culture, for example, insists that we are all 'beautiful people', 'children of the universe'. In the church, too, we tend to deny our negative feelings: 'God wants us to be happy,' 'Good Christians don't get depressed or discouraged'.

This is not biblical – and not healthy spiritually. Trying to be cheerful always can be a terrible bondage. We priests know this from the many people who come to us in secret, like Nicodemus, to tell us how angry they are, and even that they are angry with God.

Jesus was in line with the biblical tradition when he taught: 'Blessed are those who mourn, they shall be comforted.' The beatitude, like the other seven, is not speaking about events in sequence – at one time we mourn, then after a time we are comforted. It is saying that we cannot experience the comfort of grace unless we mourn. We human beings need to grieve, to 'pour out our souls before God' as the Bible often says. That is biblical spirituality, and it is freeing, like everything in the Bible.

The psalms of lament are spiritually healthy and we must learn to enter into them. It is wrong to hurry through the lamenting part of these psalms and focus on the celebration. In any case it is often impossible, since in some psalms the lament continues unrelieved to the end (e.g. 88). We must stay with the anger, bitterness and loneliness – all these things that we want to repress because our culture does not approve of them. Many people only become aware of their negative feelings when they recite a psalm.

We put a burden on people when we give them the impression that they must be on their best behaviour in the presence of God. Good parents want their children to feel free to share their feelings with them. They know that children pretend before their parents because they do not trust them.

God is being a good parent when he invites us, in the psalms of lament, to come to him as we are. Then we can ask him to save us 'for his name's sake'; our trust is in his goodness and love. We bring our anguish, discouragement even despair, and he loves us 'because of his name', his nature.

There is another dynamic at work in the psalms of lament – they help us to discover, very gradually, that beneath the negative feelings there is still trust. We might not be feeling trust right now, but we know it's there. When we profess trust, we do it humbly, not self-righteously, because we have experienced the opposite.

This is 'the truth' about ourselves that the psalms often speak of; in 17:1-2 for example: 'Lord, hear a cause that is just, no deceit is on my lips, your eyes discern the truth.' This 'truth' is part, not the whole, of ourselves. We thank God for it but not with the self-righteousness of the Pharisee.

Through praying the psalms of lament we also discover – very gradually – the fidelity of God. We make our journey to trust through anguish, fear and resentment, until we are finally able to say that his love will conquer in the end. That is a hollow, platitudinous statement if it is not the fruit of the psalms of lament. Coming at the end of a journey of lament, it is deep and touching.

Many of the images of God we get in the Bible – rescuer, redeemer, father, the one who lifts up the lowly, the defender, the rampart, the shield – come alive only within the psalms of lament. In them we celebrate the final victory of grace. Psalm 56, for example, prays: 'Have mercy on me, God, men crush me'. These men who crush us can be people, our own humanity, jealousy, lust. The psalm continues: 'When I fear I will trust in you', and further down in verse 9: 'You have kept an account of my wanderings, you have kept a record of my tears'. The psalm is inviting us to remember when we felt very great fear, and at the same time knew God would not let us down.

We can pray this psalm about what is going on in society. We think of the men who are 'crushing' our community, the poor in our society, the indebted nations of the whole world, and then make our act of trust that God's love will conquer.

One of the greatest of the psalms of lament is psalm 22 which Jesus recited on the cross. When we pray that psalm, we identify with him as he prayed it in its entirety; every line fits what he was going through. It starts with: 'My God, my God, why have you forsaken me?', but even at 4-5 there is a hint of victory: 'In you they trusted and never in vain.' This is followed by some more lament, but 23 is a full-blown prayer of celebration: 'I will tell of your name to the brethren and praise you where they are assembled.' The mood becomes even more confident in 28: 'All the earth shall remember and return to the Lord, all families of the nations shall worship before him.'

As Jesus prayed this psalm he no doubt remembered his own words: 'When I am lifted from the earth I will draw all to myself.' This is the moment when even in the midst of evil, we know that good, not evil, will conquer in the world. We think of Martin Luther King receiving the Nobel Peace Prize: 'My faith is that unarmed love will conquer in history.' That's psalm 22. Like Jesus, he was in the midst of a struggle, with no sign of victory, and yet he trusted. His faith touches us deeply because he was in a context of lament.

Through the psalms of lament, we enter into solidarity with our fellow human beings, an aspect of prayer we seem to have lost. We do pray for others, of course, but putting them in a different category from ourselves; we are here, and they are there, usually in a lower place – 'sinners', 'those less fortunate than ourselves', etc. In biblical spirituality we all share the one human condition. We intercede, not from above, but at the same level, all poor sinners, knowing weakness, finding the ability to trust, very deep within us, by the grace of God – and not always.

That is what Jesus did. He broke down barriers, reconciled all humanity, as Ephesians 2:11-18 says, by sharing our human condition. The one thing we have in common is that we know weakness at one time or another, and God took that on himself to bring us together, in union with himself. We enter that experience through the psalms of lament.

The psalms of lament teach us never to come to people from above, but to enter into their truth, knowing that it is also ours. We pray *with* people as well as *for* them. This is also the spirit of Moses' commandment to the people of Israel: 'You must not molest the stranger or oppress him, for you lived as strangers in the land of Egypt' (Ex 22:20).

A very deep spirituality indeed. We thank God for the psalms of lament.

CHAPTER 7

Psalms of Praise

The psalms of praise are celebrations of God's victories. The psalmist is elated that good has triumphed over evil. His prayer consists of joyfully telling the story of God's 'mighty deeds' – how he rescued Israel at the time of the exodus, Jerusalem from its successive enemies, individuals from all their troubles, especially David, the ideal king and symbol of the just person looked after by God.

As always in the Bible, these psalms celebrate, not 'God-in-himself' but God-doing-things – saving, rescuing, redeeming. Nowadays when we speak of God as king, we imagine him 'up there,' sitting on his throne surrounded by the angels and saints. In the Bible, we relate with God-at-work. Jesus said of him: 'My Father goes on working and so do I' (Jn 5:17). 'God is king' in the Bible is not a static statement. It means that he is accomplishing his will on the earth. 'God enthroned' is not a description of a heavenly reality. It is something happening not in heaven but on earth, his kingdom being established.

1 John 4:1 says that 'God is love, and he who lives in God lives in love'. The psalms of praise celebrate the nature of God in more active terms: 'He loves what is right, he has established equity, justice and right' (98:4). When God is king, 'the mountains bring forth peace for the people, and the hills justice' (98:3), the poor of the people will be defended, and the children of the needy saved, the oppressor crushed, 'before him the enemy shall fall' (98:7).

They pray that God's love will be shared: 'O God, give your judgement to the king, to a king's son your justice, that he may judge your people in justice, and your poor in right judgement' (71:1-2).

When God is 'judge', lowly people are respected and the false judgements of the world are overturned. God the just judge 'shall break the power of the wicked, while the strength of the just shall be exalted' (74:12). 'Let the rivers clap their hands and the hills ring out their joy, at the presence of the Lord, for he comes, he comes to rule the earth. He will rule the world with justice and the people with fairness' (97:8-9).

God's 'justice' exists when all are equal. 'Father of the orphan, defender of the widow, such is God in his holy place.' When the orphan has a father, and the widow a defender, God is in his holy place. God does not 'establish justice and right' from above: he 'lifts up the lowly from the dust, and sets them in the company of princes' (112:4).

God is 'holy' ('holy is his name') means that nobody defeats his purpose. He is not concerned about what people think; he is 'true to his name' which is lifter of the lowly, defender of the widow and the orphan. 'He sleeps not, nor slumbers, Israel's God.'

In the psalms of praise the victories of God often involve the destruction of 'enemies'. This is a very important aspect of biblical spirituality. The Bible considers goodness in the concrete, not the abstract; it looks at good people doing good things in the world. What is more, the Bible looks at the world as it is, not as it should be. People are good because they choose not to be bad, in doing good things they oppose those who do the opposite. There is no goodness without rejection of the bad, no lifting up of the lowly without casting down the mighty from their thrones.

This is very important because there is a tendency in spirituality today to ignore the real world, to speak as if we can follow Jesus without opposing the powers-that-be and causing social dislocation. The psalms keep our feet on the ground – if God is victorious then someone is defeated.

This reality does pose a problem for us. As we saw in the

previous chapter, if we are true to the teachings of Jesus we will never pray the psalms in a way which condones violence in any form, nor will we ever gloat over the defeat of our enemies.

The suggestions I made for praying the psalms of lament hold good for the psalms of praise too. One is to interpret the 'enemies' as evil tendencies, such as racism, sexism or authoritarianism, addiction in one form or another. They certainly must be defeated if God is to triumph.

Another approach is to celebrate moments when being 'brought low' is a conversion experience. When, for example, we are put to shame by the greatness of those we previously despised – those in prison, the uneducated, the vagrants – and we realise that we have to revise our values. We are 'defeated' but the defeat is a grace.

Jesus was trying to bring the chief priests and elders to that conversion in Matthew 21:28-32. They must give up their arrogance and make their way into the kingdom behind the tax collectors and prostitutes. This is the 'sacrifice' of the 'contrite spirit' of psalm 51, when the 'bones the Lord has crushed' now 'thrill' – the 'thrill' of Jesus' prayer: 'I bless you Father, Lord of heaven and earth, for hiding these things from the learned and the clever and revealing them to mere children' (Mt 11:25).

Sometimes the victories of God which we celebrate in these psalms are won without his name being mentioned. It is simply that love has conquered hatred, communion has conquered fragmentation; where once there was separation, there is now reconciliation; people – including ourselves – have become more human, more free, more in his image; they have preserved their humanity in inhuman situations.

In these psalms we also celebrate God's instruments, the saints who have won victories for him. They could be our favourite canonised ones, but also our personal saints, the great people who have touched our lives in our families and neighbourhoods, on the world stage. In the psalms of praise we tell their stories, and celebrate God at work in them.

The victories we celebrate in these psalms need not be

glorious or spectacular. They can be times when, after many failures, we (just barely!) conquered resentment or discouragement. We may want to celebrate the victory of one of our children, a friend, feeling loved for the first time, or overcoming an inferiority complex; an alcoholic or a drug addict, not in bondage any more but 'lifted up from the dung heap and set in the company of princes'.

We celebrate God's victories in a community, a parish, religious congregation, family, political movement, a nation, the world – a time when love overcame and proved itself more powerful than meanness, violence or fanaticism. God conquers when the human spirit shows that it is unconquerable, in Eastern Europe and South Africa, for example, when the oppressed continued to hope, forgive, and love.

The psalms of praise transcend time. They move from past, to present to future. That's because they are talking about God, and God is always at work, even if we cannot see him at it. So when we praise him, past, present and future are incidental. We situate ourselves wherever we want to, but are in touch with every time.

When we speak of past victories of God – 'I remember the days that are past' – we must interpret this very widely. We remember the New Testament teaching that God was at work in Jesus from the beginning of time, 'all things were created in him, through him'. In praying these psalms then, we go as far back as we want to – the past of our ethnic group, our culture, of humanity itself as it has evolved over the centuries, even in its pre-historic times. In the words of the *Magnificat,* God 'has remembered Israel' – he brings the story of our ancestors to fulfilment in us.

By praying the psalms of praise then, we become more aware of God's saving power at work in us, in the world, in history. Sometimes his presence is tangible – a Life in the Spirit seminar, a conversion experience, a family get-together, a national celebration; at other times he seems absent, but we know he is there.

Awareness of God at work is specially important in our world today. Never in the history of humanity, perhaps, has evil seemed to be more victorious, and yet we Christians are always able to see beyond evil and celebrate God's victory. 'We wait in joyful hope for the coming of our Saviour, Jesus Christ.'

The psalms of praise correct our tendency to look on prayer as a way of achieving things. There is a popular saying: 'When you have tried everything and everything has failed, try prayer.' This is a misrepresentation of the role of prayer in our lives. In this perspective it becomes an alternative source of power, to be tapped when our will or our reason has proved inadequate. The psalms of praise teach us that prayer is a different kind of activity altogether. It is a celebration of God's power, which is why Jesus said: 'Those who ask always receive, those who search always find, and those who knock will always have the door opened to them' (Lk 11:10).

No day should pass that we don't say at least one psalm of praise. The church gives us the lead by prescribing the *Magnificat* to be said every evening. No matter what the day has brought, we say with Mary (or allow her to say in us), 'My soul glorifies the Lord, my spirit rejoices in God my saviour.' Our day may have been terrible, many things may have gone wrong, but we still pray that prayer – because it is true.

We will find, then, that we begin to quieten our negative feelings and look for the presence of God where and when we did not expect to find him. That is one of the precious graces of praying the psalms of praise.

The victories we celebrate in these psalms are, of course, only partial and temporary, the 'enemies' are not finally crushed. The psalms of praise point the way towards the final victory when 'everything is subjected to Christ' and when 'the Son himself will be subject in his turn to the One who subjected all things to him so that God will be all in all' (1 Cor 15:28). From this point of view, then, the psalms of praise are also acts of hope; they express our longing: 'Come, Lord Jesus.'

CHAPTER 8

Wisdom Psalms

Wisdom psalms focus not on particular historical events but on God's overall plan for the world. They do not ask for favours; they make statements. By praying these psalms we grow to understand wisdom as the Bible does – and as God wants us to.

In recent centuries, the church has tended to neglect wisdom; we lay stress rather on keeping commandments and believing doctrines. For the Bible, however, wisdom is central to the Christian life. St Paul prays constantly that his Christians will grow in wisdom. His prayer in Ephesians 1:17 is typical: 'May the God of our Lord Jesus Christ, the Father of glory, give you a spirit of wisdom and perception of what is revealed, to bring you to full knowledge of him.'

Wisdom in the Bible corresponds to what we call today 'consciousness', 'insight', 'worldview'. It flows into right action; when we are wise we naturally and spontaneously do what is right.

The Bible never looks at reality in a static way. It looks at wisdom, too, as something we grow into through events and through meeting persons. We celebrate wisdom by remembering the journey we made to it.

We do not grow in wisdom by study or reflection; it is a precious gift of God, by which we enter into his way of seeing the world. It is God inviting us to share in his own life. Wisdom is a religious, even a contemplative, state of mind, so that, as psalm 111:10 says: 'To fear the Lord is the first stage of wisdom.' Those who receive this most precious gift are filled with joy. The Bible teaches us to celebrate wisdom with awe, like a treasure we have stumbled on without any merit on our part (Wis 7:7-14, Mt 13:4). The wisdom psalms are prayers of praise.

St Paul teaches that we grow in wisdom by 'knowing Jesus', in the biblical sense of 'knowing' – meeting at an intimate level. This gives us the important clue that we must pray the wisdom psalms with Jesus in mind, seeing him as the model of the wise person, and hearing him speak to us as the teacher of wisdom. We don't meet him in isolation but as the head of the body, the new Adam, he in whom all humanity finds its destiny. We meet him in every human being and meet everyone in him.

A good example is psalm 8 which the epistle to the Hebrews interprets as an affirmation that Jesus is the Lord of all creation (Heb 2:5-9). We can pray the psalm in praise of Jesus then, but also as a wisdom psalm, thanking God for the greatness of our human vocation as lords of creation, sharing in the Lordship of Jesus.

Identifying with Jesus is specially important when we confront the problem of suffering, the great stumbling block to wisdom. As is explained most clearly by St Paul in 1 Corinthians 1:17-25, we become wise by making a journey from falsehood to truth, from the wisdom of human beings (or of 'the world') to the wisdom of God. The highest point of the journey to wisdom is when we accept the crucified Christ. Wisdom is true if it can 'express the crucifixion of Christ' (v. 17).

The 'wisdom of the world' fails the test. St Paul quotes Is 29:14: 'I shall destroy the wisdom of the wise and bring to nothing all the learning of the learned', and draws the conclusion that 'God's foolishness is wiser than human wisdom.'

The psalmist often recounts his journey to God's wisdom. Examples are psalms 49, 73 and 77. He rebels when he sees the upright persecuted and sinners prosper. He is persuaded only gradually to recognise that God still rules the world. It is the journey of Jesus in the Garden of Gethsemane, as expressed in Hebrews 5:7: 'During his life on earth, he offered up prayer and entreaty, aloud and in silent tears, to the one who had power to save him out of death. Although he was Son, he learnt to obey through suffering.'

In times of tragedy, personal or national, we too feel that there is no logic to life, we demand miracles like the Jews, look for human wisdom like the Greeks (cf 1 Cor 1:22). In praying these wisdom psalms we identify with the psalmist, with Jesus on the cross, with the Corinthians; we thank God for the times we have made the journey and pray for the grace to make it again in the future.

Sometimes the psalmist comes to a rational conclusion, for example, 'that wise men and fools must both perish and leave their wealth to others' (49:11). At other times, like Job and Jesus, wisdom is making a blind act of trust in God: 'Into your hands I commend my spirit.'

Sometimes our journey into wisdom starts from a feeling of discouragement at how pervasive and how powerful evil is. The psalmist, too, often wonders at the pervasiveness of evil but then works his way to celebrating the greater power of God. Psalm 14, verses 2 to 3, paints a very gloomy picture. 'From heaven the Lord looks down' and sees only sin: 'All have left the right path, depraved, every one.' Verse 5 recognises: 'See how they tremble with fear, for God is with the just.'

Psalm 36 also reflects on the power of evil: 'In his (the sinner's) mouth are mischief and deceit, all wisdom is gone' and then 'he plots the defeat of goodness as he lies on his bed'. Then it remembers that God's grace is even more powerful: 'Your love, Lord, reaches to heaven; your truth to the skies.' We think of St Paul's exclamation: 'God has imprisoned all in their own disobedience only to show mercy to all' (Rom 11:32).

Over the centuries, Christian theologians have taken the biblical message as a starting point from which they have arrived at different insights – doctrines, philosophy, ethics and so on. These insights are not found explicitly in the wisdom psalms but are implied. It is up to us to integrate them into our prayer of the psalms.

Psalm 50, for example, is a meditation on virtue as something interior. It rejects the idea that God is pleased with our exterior actions. When we read the psalm we should hear in it the voice of Jesus, especially the sermon on the mount, Mt 5:26-37. We must go further. Modern psychology has hepled us to uncover the many subtle ways in which we human beings can cover up our faults. Under the guise of 'humility' we can be running away from our responsibilities and the possibility of failure; what we call 'patience' can be playing the role of victim; 'zeal' for God can be a desire for power or revenge.

In praying psalm 50 we recognise these ways in which we 'recite God's commandments and take his covenant on our lips', but very subtly, often unconsciously, 'despise his law and throw his words to the winds'.

Psalm 8, as we have seen, celebrates the dignity of the human person as Lord of the universe. Today, because of the insights of great educators like Paulo Freire, we are conscious that the education system encourages passivity; it frustrates God's plan for humanity. True education makes students aware that 'God has made them little less than gods' and 'crowned them with honour and glory'. We pray psalm 8 as a celebration of Paulo Freire's contribution to the wisdom of our age.

On the other hand, we are conscious today that Christians have misinterpreted the biblical theme of human authority over nature. The Genesis text, 'fill the earth and conquer it' (1:28), has been interpreted to mean that human beings can treat nature as they please, abuse it even, which has brought us to the environmental crisis of our time. In praying psalm 8, we celebrate Jesus' way of being Lord of the universe. The Father gave him 'power over the works of his hand' but he exercised this power humbly and in a spirit of service.

I have been speaking in this chapter of wisdom psalms. I remind you, however, of what I said in an earlier chapter, that the psalms cannot be put into water-tight compartments. It often happens that in the midst of a psalm of praise or one of lament, the psalmist utters an exclamation of joy and wonder at the wisdom of God.

It happens to us in our prayer too that in the midst of a prayer of petition or of thanksgiving we are struck by an insight. The psalms teach us that when this happens, we should interrupt the flow of our prayer, spend some time articulating this insight, and thank God for it. Doing it with the psalms we will be constantly celebrating God's gift of wisdom – and 'grow in the perception of what is revealed', until we come 'to the full knowledge of him'.

CHAPTER 9

The Psalms and Contemplative Prayer

In chapter 5, I explained how, through *lectio divina,* we come to the point where we pray the psalms contemplatively. I would like to reflect further on psalms as a way of contemplation.

Contemplation is first of all an interior attitude but it must be expressed and nourished by moments when we say: 'I am engaged in contemplative prayer.' We don't have to use the word; thousands of church members have never heard the word and pray contemplatively. Nor must we make a fuss over these moments. They are important not in themselves but only because they foster the contemplative attitude.

Having made this clear, we must recognise that contemplative moments are precious, and we as a church should spend more time speaking about them, celebrating them, and helping one another come to them.

Psalm 5 provides a good starting point for understanding how to pray the psalms contemplatively, since it speaks about entering trustingly into the presence of God.

The psalmist starts by praying to God to bring him into his presence. He prays humbly, since he is conscious of being in a situation of sin. 'To my words give ear, O Lord, give heed to my groaning, attend to the sound of my cries ... it is you whom I invoke ... watching and waiting.'

He knows very well how undeserving he is of entering God's presence: 'You are no God who loves evil, no sinner is your guest ... you hate all who do evil, you destroy all who lie.' We can paraphrase: 'I know I don't deserve to be in your presence, I am so destructive because of my jealousy, lust and resentment, so afraid to face up to the truth of myself.'

The psalmist trusts in God's love, however. 'But I,' he says (note how always in the Bible sinfulness does not define a person, it is not 'I'; 'I' is the goodness within us, our true self), 'through the greatness of your love, I have access to your house, I bow down before your holy temple, filled with awe' – a perfect description of the moment of contemplative prayer.

Then the psalmist changes mood again; he remembers the many things in himself that block contemplation: 'Lead me, Lord, in your justice, because of those who lie in wait.' There are indeed all kinds of enemies 'lying in wait' to ambush us on our journey to contemplation – spiritual ambition, self-righteousness, escapism.

The psalmist prays that God will overcome them all: 'Lord, make clear your way before me. No truth can be found in their mouths, their heart is all mischief, their throat a wide open grave, all honey their speech.' How true it is that when we want to pray, sin plays tricks on us – self-deceit, pretentiousness, hiding behind holy language. 'Declare them guilty, O God, let them fail in their designs … they have defied you.'

The psalmist concludes by renewing his trust: 'All those you protect shall be glad … you shelter them, in you they rejoice' – he has entered into contemplation.

This then is the journey to contemplation which we make humbly but confidently, knowing that 'because of the greatness of God's love', we have 'access to his house'. This is an important point because our church's rich teaching on contemplative prayer, though better known than it was some years ago, is still not being shared with most of its members. They do not in fact 'have access' to this most sacred room in 'his house' and as a result are vulnerable to the traps which 'lie in wait' – the various wrong tendencies I have spoken about, which can all be traced back to a neglect of contemplation.

Contemplation cannot be planned. It comes to us like a gift; it is only 'through the greatness of God's love' that we 'bow down before his holy temple filled with awe'. This is important because of the modern tendency which I mentioned earlier, of trying to regiment or over-organise our prayer life; this tendency becomes more harmful as we go deeper into prayer. We dispose ourselves for contemplation, exteriorly and interiorly, but after that we 'watch and wait'.

The contemplative moment often comes not when we are in a church or before the Blessed Sacrament, but when we are going about our daily duties. People think they must fix a 'time for meditation' but this is not possible for many people today, especially lay men and women, busy with young children, living in noisy neighbourhoods, having to rush to and from work. The Rule of St Benedict does not fix a 'time' when the community must engage in contemplative prayer as became the custom in later religious orders. He knew that prayer is not something that can be organised; it emerges when and where it will – or God wills.

This is not to say that it is not helpful to have fixed times for prayer. Indeed many find them necessary, especially those who lead very active lives, constantly using will and reason. But the individual must decide which is the suitable time. We can add that having our place for contemplative prayer close to where we live most of our day is a good thing. So too our times for prayer should not be too far removed from times of activity. All this helps to bring about the Benedictine integration of work and prayer as two moments of union with God.

When we pray the psalms contemplatively we start from reality. This is crucial. One of the 'enemies', always 'lying in wait' to ambush our prayer, is escapism. One of the great problems for spirituality today is separating relationship with God from relationship with the world. In biblical contemplative prayer, we don't leave our reality but go deeper and deeper into it – like Jesus reciting psalm 22 on the cross.

If we say, 'Lord, I am very upset, but I want to forget that, so that I can enter into your presence', we are saying that God is not with us when we are upset – or with the person who upsets us. We cannot then be in union with God because we have left part of ourselves out of the relationship. Contemplation is always an experience of integration, 'bowing down in awe before God's holy temple'. Sometimes we may need to integrate parts of ourselves we have been running away from for a long time – failures we have not accepted, people we haven't forgiven.

There has been a tendency in our church for the past few centuries to play down contemplative experiences – a good thing if it means not exaggerating their importance. But celebrating these moments, as our tradition teaches us to, is spiritually healthy; we remember to thank God for these precious graces; memories of times when we experienced God deeply help us to cope with difficult moments; we can look critically at these experiences to protect ourselves from being ambushed by those 'who lie in wait'.

Any psalm, once we enter deeply into it, can lead us to contemplative prayer, so we should not categorise some as 'more contemplative' than others. However, some psalms are more easily interpreted as celebrations of contemplation and it is good, now and then, to pray them from this perspective.

Psalm 27 is entitled, in the Grail edition, 'Triumphant trust in God.' The psalmist is going through a bad time, 'evil-doers draw near', but he is confident that he will draw close to the Lord: 'There is one thing I ask of the Lord, for this I long, to live in the house of the Lord all the days of my life … he hides me in the shelter of his tent … and I shall offer within his tent a sacrifice of joy' (27:4-5). This is going to happen perfectly in heaven, but it also happens in contemplation which, in our tradition, is considered a foreshadowing of heaven.

Psalm 42 follows a similar pattern. The exile is nostalgic for God's presence: 'My soul is thirsting for God … my tears have become my bread'; as he 'pours out his soul', the memories come back: 'How I would lead the rejoicing crowd into the house of God, amid cries of gladness.' He concludes: 'Why are you cast down, my soul, why groan within me? Hope in God, I will praise him still.' When we feel in a 'far country', as we all do at times, we remember that we have been in the house of God.

In the psalms which celebrate Jerusalem, the city can be a symbol of contemplative moments. Contemplation is the Jerusalem within us, the holy city, the sacred space where we are at home in the deepest and most true part of ourselves, in the presence of God and of all humanity. Psalm 48 can be a celebration of how, in that inner Jerusalem, we are safe from the many foes which surround us but cannot enter.

Psalm 95 is the daily call to prayer for those who say *The Prayer of the Church*. The first stanza sets the tone. It invites us to forget ourselves and leave everything in God's hands: 'Come ring out our joy to the Lord, hail the rock who saves us.' We think only of God, our rock, the dependable one.

The second stanza looks at creation: 'A mighty God is the Lord, a great king above all gods.' The depths of the earth are in his hands, the high mountains are his, our beautiful sea belongs to him for he made it; the dry land was shaped by his hands. We don't close our eyes, we look around us, at the sea, the mountains, the dry land.

The third stanza invites us to cast off our dissatisfaction at ourselves and 'come in' to God's presence. We enter, 'bow and bend low' – no activity – 'kneel before the God who made us', aware that 'he is our God, and we the people who belong to his pasture, the sheep of his flock.' No conditions are laid down; we come just as we are, 'led by his hand'.

Then the psalm takes a very human turn. God says, 'I know you are resisting. You're saying, "Lord I trust you," but you wonder if I am really going to see you through.' He exclaims, 'Oh that today you would listen to my voice!'

Meribah and Massah were places where the Israelites, having come through the Red Sea, looked ahead, saw the wilderness and said they were going back to Egypt. Don't look on them with scorn, the psalm says, you are like them, 'they are your fathers.'

'For forty years I was wearied of these people ... these people do not know my ways...' This is very touching. Thomas Merton describes contemplative prayer as being 'totally dependent on God's mercy'. That's the sentiment here. We know God is tired of us and we say: 'Lord, I know you are right to be frustrated with us, but please give us another chance, still let us enter your rest.'

Psalm 95 is very true to life – no pretence, no leaving of reality, we really come to God 'just as we are'. That's biblical contemplative prayer.

CHAPTER 10

Nature in the Psalms

Our church has not been playing much of a role in solving the world's ecological crisis, and part of the reason is that our spiritual formation does little to foster a healthy attitude to nature. In most countries of the world, lessons in ecology do not form part of First Communion or Confirmation programmes. It is not a topic for Sunday sermons. In our church's tradition, a person can be deeply prayerful and have no feel for nature.

If we go back to our spiritual roots, however, which means in practice back to the Bible, we find that our true tradition is deeply ecological. Praying the psalms will help us recover this aspect of our tradition. It won't happen spontaneously. After centuries of neglect, we must make a conscious effort to get in touch with the biblical approach to nature.

The key concept is that we human beings are in communion with nature. We have a common origin since we were 'fashioned of dust from the soil' (Gen 2:7) and we share a common destiny: 'Creation still retains the hope of being freed like us from its slavery to decadence, to enjoy the same freedom and glory as the children of God' (Rom 8:23).

Anthropologists divide religions according to how God reveals himself in them – in history or in the cosmos. Some tend to be historical, others cosmic. Islam, for example, is based on God's revelation to a historical person, the prophet Mohammed. The African religions tend to discover God in natural phenomena – the sun, the rain, thunder, trees. The God of the Bible, especially as interpreted in our Catholic tradition, reveals himself in both history and nature.

Easter, for example, celebrates (in the northern hemisphere) an event of nature, the passing from winter to spring, and at the same time a historical event, God's rescuing of the Israelites from the Egyptians, and raising Jesus from the dead. Christmas, too, celebrates two events, the winter equinox, when the sun begins its return to the north, and the historical birth of Jesus. God sends the sun into the heavens in the middle of winter and sends Jesus as light in the darkness.

Our liturgical 'seasons' refer to times in nature and in the historical life of Jesus. Nature determined the date of Christmas and the church turned it into a historical feast. The church's private devotions also make the link between history and the cosmos: the 'beautiful month of May' for example, is dedicated to Mary the 'beautiful person'.

The God of the Bible is consistent, he acts according to fixed patterns whether in nature or in history in the same way. Jesus' nature parables are in line with this understanding. We learn (and celebrate) how God acts by 'considering' (not merely looking at) the birds of the sky, a sower sowing, a seed sprouting spontaneously with the farmer not even knowing it's happening. In nature, personal spiritual growth, family life, human history, he always brings light out of darkness, starts small, achieves things non-violently.

Because God is consistent, we can praise him at any level of his work and be in touch with all the levels. We don't have to make the link explicit. When, for example, we thank God for a beautiful tree, we are thanking him for all his creation, natural and human, and for all those who collaborate with him in his work of creation.

God's creation (in nature and history) is harmonious and abundant, the two going together since any form of disharmony blocks abundance. In our modern languages, we refer to 'might is right' as the 'law of the jungle', but this is a misnomer. The jungle is, in fact, a place of harmony within infinite variety and therefore of great abundance.

The Bible teaches that our human actions affect the rest of

creation, naturally since we are in communion with it. When we live in harmony with one another and with nature, the human community is prosperous and nature is bountiful; when we live selfishly, there is a general breakdown at every level.

We must interpret this biblical teaching correctly. Many natural disasters are really 'acts of God'. But many disasters (some would say most) are, even if remotely, the result of human wrong doing – deforestation, dams, soil erosion, abuse of pesticides, civil strife, poor housing. When, therefore, we pray in a psalm for bountiful crops, we are also praying for harmonious relationships in the community. Psalm 103 celebrates the bounty of creation and then concludes: 'Let sinners vanish from the earth and the wicked exist no more' (v. 35).

God's work of creation (both in nature and history) is continuous. He is always creating the world anew, restoring its harmony and abundance. The Jews took this notion of continuous creation for granted; it fitted their understanding of the universe. For them water was the first reality. At creation God separated the water from the dry land, lifted up one body of water and put the vault of heaven to keep it there, and pressed down the rest beneath the earth. The problem for them was that the water was always threatening to take over again, which was what happened at the deluge, and only God's power, his continuous creation, was keeping it back.

When the psalms thank God for creation, then, they are referring to his continuous intervention by which he keeps the water at bay, above the firmament and beneath the dry land.

We do not accept the biblical cosmology, but we can enter into its language since modern science too sees creation as continuous. The universe as a whole, and every part within it, is in constant motion, with forces of integration and of fragmentation contending against each other. The world continues to exist as we know it because the integration force is stronger, and for us believers that is the work of God, the creator.

Because we are in communion with God's entire work of creation, the human community (and each individual within it) is also a battleground between forces of reconciliation – love, forgiveness, compassion – and fragmentation – selfishness, the desire for revenge, ambition. We too survive because God continues his work of creation, and in the Bible we praise him for it.

The biblical world is a communion, but there is a hierarchy of being. We humans are made in the image and likeness of God and, therefore, have a higher level of being than the animals and inanimate nature. It is not a relationship of domination, still less of conquest, but of service. Our role is to 'cultivate and take care of' God's bountiful garden (Gen 2:15).

Nature is voiceless, it praises God by being. Our role as human beings is to articulate its praise, to be its priests. 'In the name of every creature under heaven, we praise God's glory as we say holy, holy, holy' (Eucharistic Prayer 4). This priestly role is wonderfully expressed in the canticle of the three young men (Daniel 3:37-88), not a psalm in the strict sense, but said in the psalter at Morning Prayer on every second Sunday and on all feast days. We 'priests' do not of course lose contact with nature; we praise God with natural instruments like 'drums and strings'.

The Bible, and especially the psalms, invite us to enter into our dignity as the priests of the universe, to be conscious of thunder and lightning, the great mountains and rivers of the world, its seas, praising God in us. We are a 'royal priesthood', which means that we not only offer worship but we walk the earth as Adam walked in the garden, with awe but without fear.

Praying in communion with nature, we are in communion with Jesus, the 'first-born of all creation'. We must learn to experience him at work in the movements of nature, wherever darkness conquers light, a small seed gradually becomes a great tree, harmony emerges out of diversity.

The church seems to like psalm 147:12-20. It occurs twice

in the weekly psalter (in that numbering 148). The psalmist invites the inhabitants of Jerusalem to praise God for what he has done for them: 'He established peace on your borders, and he feeds you with finest wheat.' Note the link. God's people reap the finest wheat and they live at peace with their neighbours.

'He sends out his word to the earth, he scatters hoar frost like ashes. He hurls down hailstones like crumbs, at his word, the waters flow.' They have energising cold weather, and when they're tired of the cold, God breathes again, the ice melts and they have plenty of water to drink.

At the end, the psalm says: 'He has not dealt thus with other nations.' If we are not God's people, we have famine and all kinds of shortages. Where there is respect for creation – the body, the soil, the trees, God, people – there is abundance at every level.

Psalm 33 starts with a joyful celebration of the Creator: 'By his word the heavens were made, by the breath of his mouth all the stars, he collects the waves of the ocean, he stores up the depths of the sea' (33:6-7), and then moves on to celebrate God's intervention in history: 'He frustrates the designs, he defeats the plans of the peoples' (33:10).

Psalm 8 starts with universal praise. 'Your Majesty is praised above the heavens, on the lips of children and of babes ... You have found praise to foil your enemy, to silence the foe and the rebel.' Everybody is praising God; all disharmony is gone.

'What is man that you should keep him in mind, mortal man that you care for him? Yet you have made him little less than a god, put all things under his feet.' Note the good order. Everything in its place, humanity subject to God, and exercising authority over the earth.

Psalm 19: 'The heavens proclaim the glory of God and the firmament shows forth the work of his hand. Day unto day takes up the story and night unto night makes known the message. No speech, no word, no voice is heard, yet their span extends through all the earth, their words to the utmost bounds of the world.'

St Paul applies this psalm to the preaching of the gospel in Romans 10:18. He invites us to make the link between nature and human behaviour: 'No speech, no word, no voice is heard' is true of nature's way of proclaiming God's glory and it is also true of human beings. Their most effective message is their example. No speech, no word, no voice is heard as they proclaim the glory of God.

The psalm then celebrates the sun: 'There he has placed a tent for the sun. It comes forth like a bridegroom coming from his tent, rejoices like a champion to run its course.' We celebrate all those who bring life to the world – the sun, God, the courageous people of Eastern Europe, of South Africa, Jesus. They are all one in doing God's work.

Psalm 92 meditates on trees 'still bearing fruit when they are old, still full of sap, still green.' We celebrate an old samaan tree in the savannah, and at the same time our old granny, the church with all its faults, Jesus on the cross, all of them 'still full of sap, still green'. We are in communion with them all – nature, history, individuals, societies, the human family. That's biblical prayer!

CHAPTER 11

The Psalms as Political Prayer

One of the important developments in the life of the church in recent years has been the emergence of 'political spirituality'.

Thomas Merton noted this development: 'The real way to spiritual renewal today is precisely where you would least expect it: in the field of political life. It is here that all the crucial struggles and temptations of our time have to be faced.'

Merton meant 'political life' in a broad sense, not merely party politics or government, but public life in any form. 'Political spirituality' is, therefore, the logical development of lay spirituality, which can be defined as the capacity to have a deep relationship with God and at the same time be fully citizens of the world. Those who follow that path are committed to making society more like what God wants it to be. It is normal that some of them will get involved in public life, and the rest of the church must be in solidarity with them.

A political spirituality will naturally be rooted in prayer, and this will include praying the psalms. We need to develop in our church, therefore, the practice of praying the psalms from our experience of public life. This will not be our only, nor necessarily our main, perspective – we must let the psalms express our sentiments in every area of human living. But we should adopt the political perspective from time to time.

The key to developing a lay spirituality is consciousness of 'the kingdom of God'. This is a biblical expression meaning the world as God originally planned it, how he still wants it to be, how it would be if it were totally under his rule, how he is actually forming it in small, partial ways, until it is finally established. The 'kingdom' was the goal of Jesus' life, what he lived and died for. Jesus did not preach himself (he would not be a good model if he did) but 'the kingdom of God'.

The Bible is very clear on what the kingdom looks like. Isaiah 11:1-11 is probably the best description of it. The kingdom is a place of harmony and abundance, where the humble feel safe, and there is harmony between human beings and God, between human beings themselves, between them and the animal kingdom, and within the animal kingdom.

By praying the psalms with the kingdom in mind, we gradually 'take on the mind of Jesus'. Like him we long for the world to be more like the kingdom; thank God for those who are making the world like the kingdom; commit ourselves to playing our part in the process, without violence since it is the work of God.

In order to pray the psalms in this way, we must be concrete, situate ourselves in our political situation, the world or our country as it really is. We can then, in the words of the psalms, celebrate the positive aspects of our modern world – its stress on human rights, on equality for women and minority groups, solidarity between rich and poor nations. We ask God's forgiveness for the negatives – international debt, the iniquitous trade system, abuses of human rights. As always with the psalms, our prayer will be linked to events and persons who symbolise grace (praise) and evil (lament).

Our experiences of the kingdom in public life are always limited. The victories are temporary and partial, with some ambiguous aspects. We must be conscious of this, so that our reading is not naïve. Certain political events and people do, however, fill us with very great hope and joy and we should therefore celebrate them as experiences of the kingdom.

In chapter 9, I showed how even though every psalm can be prayed contemplatively, the Jerusalem psalms are specially suitable to celebrate contemplation. So too, while every psalm can be interpreted as of the kingdom, those that speak of Jerusalem lend themselves most easily to this interpretation since the 'holy city' is an important symbol of the kingdom in the Bible.

Psalm 118 is a good example. It is a psalm we are specially encouraged to love, since in *The Prayer of the Church* it is said every Sunday, either at morning prayer or in the prayer during the day. It is a song of praise, accompanying a warrior as he enters triumphantly into Jerusalem after a victory.

It was prayed many times in the history of the Jewish people, but for us Christians is always a celebration of Jesus' victorious entry into Jerusalem. In all four gospels, the story is told in the words of this psalm – together with Zechariah 9. Ever since then, whatever victory of grace we Christians celebrate, we are also celebrating Jesus' entry into Jerusalem.

It was a moment of victory because he had remained faithful. All his years in his public ministry he had loved and had forgiven. He had had to resist those who opposed him – the temptations of the devil in the wilderness; Peter's 'temptation' that he must not go to Jerusalem; the attempts of the Pharisees to stop him eating with publicans and sinners. He knew the leaders in Jerusalem were plotting to kill him, but refused to confront them with 'horses and chariots' or with 'the bow of war'. He entered the city on his own terms.

We can make the psalm our own by celebrating some 'political' victory which has moved us deeply. It could be one on the world stage, like Gandhi bringing a temporary end to violence, the end of apartheid, the end of the civil war in Mozambique, the launch of the peace process between Israel and the Palestinians. It could also be a local victory – a better deal for workers, the coming to power of a radical political movement, the recognition of a trade union.

Since we are praying imaginatively we must situate ourselves concretely, by celebrating a specific moment which symbolised the triumph of grace – the day Mandela was released from prison, Good Friday 1998 in Belfast, the handshake between Rabin and Yasser Arafat, Rosa Parks finally winning the battle against segregation in Alabama, the fall of the Berlin Wall. We walk with the victors in procession to God's temple.

In verses 2 to 4, we invite all peoples to praise God with us. The 'sons of Israel' are the church, the 'sons of Aaron' are people of prayer, 'those who fear the Lord' are all men and women of goodwill. We think of the universal acclaim for the great victories of the human spirit in our century.

In verses 5 to 14, we remember the hard times the warrior went through – defenders of democracy in Chile tortured and imprisoned, water hoses turned on civil rights workers, Mordechai Vanu imprisoned for revealing Israel's nuclear secrets.

Verses 19 to 29 describe the climatic moment when the victor makes his grand entry into the holy place. It is in the form of a dialogue:

19 to 21: the victor calls with (moral) authority on the temple officials to open the gates for him;

22 to 27: the temple officials (or perhaps the bystanders) welcome him with very great joy ('grant us salvation' is the 'hosanna' of the crowds on the first Palm Sunday);

28 to 29: the victor speaks again.

This is a liturgical moment, but it is a 'liturgy of life' like the judgement scene in Mt 25:31-46. We celebrate a new political leader taking office, an exile returning in glory, a wrongly accused finally reinstated. 'The stone rejected by the builders became the corner stone' reminds us of Churchill calling Gandhi a 'half-naked khafir', the military regime in Brazil deciding that Archbishop Helder Camara would become a 'non-person', freedom fighters called 'terrorists'.

Celebrating these great historical moments fills us with hope that, even in this world, truth conquers eventually and so the future is safe in the hands of God.

CHAPTER 12

Praying Psalm 23

I would like to propose a practical lesson on praying psalm 23, the Good Shepherd psalm, one of the best known and most loved in the psalter. It is a wisdom psalm since it does not ask for anything, but makes statements about the workings of grace in the world.

My purpose is to help you pray it well and also to experience how infinitely adaptable this psalm is. As always, it is your experience that must determine how it will come alive for you, so you must situate yourself concretely before it.

Ask yourself first, who is the shepherd you want to celebrate in the psalm – friend, family member, neighbour, fellow-worker, priest, teacher. It may be God himself who has been a good shepherd to you, blessed you, consoled you. It might be someone else's experience of the good shepherd that you want to celebrate, one of your children, a friend, someone you read about in the newspaper or saw on television. The shepherd might be yourself in your role as parent, friend, spiritual guide, employer.

You must decide whether the shepherd is someone who cares for individuals or a community leader – the leader of a neighbourhood, a nation, a church community, a culture, humanity. Is the shepherd a collective person, the church, a political movement, an NGO?

Remember Jesus of the gospels, 'fulfilled' in all these shepherds. See him pastoring his disciples, the tax collectors and sinners, the good thief on the cross, Mary of Magdala on Easter Sunday morning, the twelve in the upper room.

Whatever the memory, it must be of a concrete event by

which the shepherd showed himself or herself to be 'good'. You will then have to locate yourself in time – present, past or future. The present: 'Now I am in turmoil, but this psalm is reminding me of where the shepherd is leading me.' The past: 'When I read this psalm I remember what happened when a shepherd was there for me.' The future: 'Lord, I don't see this psalm happening in my experience, but I am praying that you will send me a good shepherd.'

You might want to read it as a call to conversion: 'Forgive me (or us), Lord, that I (or we) have not been the shepherd described in this psalm.'

Enter into the movement of the psalm, starting in one place but seeing it in the context of the entire psalm. When you have grasped it as a whole, you will find that you want to 'rest' in one section. This is the contemplative moment in your prayer.

Stanza 1

The first verse does not have much for the imagination, so you can move to the second: 'Fresh and green are the pastures where he gives me repose; near restful waters he leads me to revive my drooping spirit.' The parallelism is progressive since there is movement from the first half to the second, and the metaphor changes. Take time to enter deeply into each image, taking one at a time – repose in pastures that are fresh and green, and then drooping spirits revived in restful waters.

Let the concrete memories surface – 'last week my spirit was drooping, but this shepherd led me to restful waters', or feel a great longing for the passage to come true: 'Lord, the spirit of our community is drooping, send us a shepherd to lead us to restful waters.' Feel the call to conversion: 'Lord, I have not noticed that student; his spirit is drooping but I have not led him to restful waters.'

Stanza 2

The image moves in a new direction. The sheep have left the

green pastures and the restful waters and set out on a journey. It is a dangerous journey, with many 'wrong paths' and at a certain point they must 'walk in the valley of darkness'. Let the image touch you, get a feel for the dark, and then the shepherd's crook and staff guiding the sheep along the right path. Spend some time on 'he is true to his name', a touching image of 'the reliable one', who we know won't let us down.

Let the images stir up feelings of gratitude, repentance, petition. See your country, or modern humanity, moving into uncharted waters and yearning for competent, caring leaders.

Stanza 3

As often in the psalms, the pronouns change without warning. In the first two stanzas, the shepherd was 'he', but is now 'you'.

The image changes radically. There are no longer sheep, but human beings enjoying a great banquet, with 'overflowing cups', and in festive garments, 'my head anointed with oil'. Let new memories surface – rest after a long and dangerous road, a moment of unlimited festivity. Celebrate times of grace – of spiritual renewal, a Life-in-the-Spirit seminar for example; spouses reconciled after years of turmoil; national peace after long, tense negotiations, guided by a wise and patient leader.

'In the sight of my foes' is very touching. Imagine the scene. The foes are there, looking on, but powerless. We think of Jesus on the cross with the chief priests and elders jeering him, Mandela harshly treated in prison, times when we ourselves have ignored criticisms and persevered in a noble quest.

Stanza 4

The image moves again. It is journey's end. All is at peace. There are no foes 'in sight'.

It can be literally an end-of-time moment, a place where the wanderer will dwell 'for ever and ever'. 'All the days of my life' refers then to the 'world without end' of heaven, the 'long

life' promised to the servant of the Lord in Isaiah 53:10. The
stanza celebrates the entry of the just person into heaven after
a long and painful illness, after persecution or many disappointments; Jesus ascending to the right hand of the Father;
Mary assumed into heaven.

But you can also apply the stanza to temporary resting
places, deeply satisfying victories of grace when we say with
gratitude: 'Thank God the struggle is over, never again'; a
moment of contemplative prayer; peace in the home; the end
of a long and destructive war. The moment doesn't last;
disappointments follow but they do not cloud the memory.
It remains a source of hope that 'goodness and kindness follow us all the days of our life'.

APPENDIX

The Psalms divided into categories

The psalms are listed below according to the three categories proposed in chapter 5: praise, lament and wisdom. Readers are reminded, however, that the psalms are free, spontaneous responses to particular experiences and cannot be fitted neatly into categories. There is much overlapping; the psalmist mixes praise and lamentation, his insights into wisdom lead to (or emerge from) praise, and sometimes lament. It is often difficult to decide which category a psalm should be put into. With this reservation, some people still find the categories helpful.

Lament: 3, 4, 5, 6, 7, 12, 13, 14, 17, 22, 25, 26, 28, 31, 35, 38, 39, 40, 41, 42, 44, 51, 54, 55, 56, 57, 58, 59, 61, 69, 70, 72, 74, 79, 80, 83, 88, 102, 108, 109, 120, 123, 130, 131, 137, 139, 140, 141, 142, 143, 144.

Praise: 16, 18, 20, 21, 23, 27, 29, 30, 32, 33, 43, 45, 46, 47, 48, 60, 63, 64, 65, 66, 67, 68, 71, 75, 76, 81, 85, 86, 87, 92, 93, 95, 96, 97, 98, 99, 100, 103, 104, 105, 106, 107, 113, 114, 115, 116, 117, 118, 122, 124, 126, 129, 134, 135, 136, 138, 147, 148, 149, 150.

Wisdom: 1, 2, 8, 9-10, 11,15, 19, 24, 34, 36, 37, 49, 50, 52, 53, 62, 73, 77, 78, 82, 84, 89, 90, 91, 94, 101, 110, 111, 112, 119, 121, 125, 127, 128, 132, 133, 145, 146.